BORN TO BE GREAT
Remarkable
Exceptional
Awesome
Terrific,
DIE EMPTY

Keys to Unlock
Your Greatness

Life Coaching Journal

TSHEPISO MALEDU

authorHOUSE®

AuthorHouse™ UK
1663 Liberty Drive
Bloomington, IN 47403 USA
www.authorhouse.co.uk
Phone: 0800.197.4150

Published by AuthorHouse 09/14/2017

ISBN: 978-1-5246-8292-7 (sc)
ISBN: 978-1-5246-8291-0 (e)

CONTENTS

FOREWORD

I've had the pleasure of being friends with the author for the past seven years. This has afforded me the opportunity of watching her live the contents of this book daily as she has established herself as a coach and sought after public speaker. Tshepiso is multitalented and driven, this book eloquently infuses her multifaceted persona through lessons shared as steps to finding success in this book. The contents are a combination of theoretical knowledge she has gained from her academic qualifications and practically tried and tested lessons she has gained through her life's journey. One of the things I most admire is her decision to choose to use her toughest life experiences as lessons from which she could draw knowledge to share with others. She is driven by the desire to see others fulfil their potential and the birth of this book is evidence of that commitment.

This book is a journey to fulfil purpose and the greatness that abides within all of us. If you've aspired to be more in life, if you've dreamed of living out your true potential, if you've been asking yourself what difference your life can make and wondering how you would achieve that, then you've picked up the right book! The words in these pages are for you. In this book are the tools and strategies I have watched Tshepiso use to reach her goals over and over again. The best part is that the dream of ultimate life success is not for the few it is a possibility for us all, and can be a reality for you. So keep turning the pages. It only gets better ☺

I experienced this book as a tool that caused me to pause, reflect and assess my own goals. It challenged me to entrench discipline when it comes to going after my own goals, it also reminded me that I am alive for a purpose and engaging in its pursuance would bring fulfilment. I believe that it will do that for you too! I am so excited by the birth of this book and I know that as your read it, action the points and follow the steps your life will change and you will live GREAT!

Lindelwe Nxumalo – Social Development Practitioner and Editor

WHY BORN TO BE GREAT?

We are all born with the potential to be great; however there are certain things that hinder us from being great. This journal is meant to help you discover the greatness inside and provide you with tools that will help you succeed. It is meant to help you introspect, reflect and take action.

Dr Myles Munroe once said the richest place on earth is not the gold and diamond mines of South Africa, the richest place on earth is the graveyard because buried beneath the soil are books that were not written, ideas that were not shared, songs that were not sung, and purpose that was not fulfilled. Die empty is using all the potential that is inside of us before we die.

NUGGETS

The book uses bite size inspirational nuggets to learn principles, great thoughts to reflect on and self - coaching question to think about and journal.

Description
Inspirational Nuggets Learn bite size inspirational principles
Great Thoughts These are key take aways from the topic. The thoughts noted are to inspire and motivate you to achieve your full and true potential.
Self-Coaching Questions Reflection is key to growth as an individual. Take time to read and reflect on these self-coaching questions. The questions are intended to guide you to achieving your potential.

1

DISCOVER YOUR GREAT POTENTIAL

Each and every person is born with the potential to be GREAT

Someone once said when we are born, we are born with our hands closed symbolising that we are holding something in our hands and when we die our hands are opened symbolising that we have used everything that we had.

You were born in this time and generation for a purpose and a reason. You need to discover, why you are alive now!

I use a certain illustration in my presentations. I hold up a R100 note in my hand and I ask the people who want the note. Most people will raise their hands and say they want the R100 note. I then squash the R100 note in my hand, making sure to shrink it, and ask if there is still anyone who wants it. A few hands go down but most people still raise their hands.

I then take the R100 note and put it under my armpit, and then I ask again. The numbers of hands drop a bit as people react to my actions. I then take it a step further, I take the R100 note and put it in my mouth, this time around fewer hands remain raised as others look on disgusted. I then ask those whose hands are still raised why they still want the R100 note. They respond saying that the **value of the R100 note does not change** no matter what I do to it and so they still want it. No matter what I did to the note. It did not change its value.

It's the same thing with you; each of us is valuable. We all have value when we are born, but our upbringing and circumstances can make us feel as if we are not valuable anymore.

No matter what has happened to you and what life throws at you (being crushed, called names, abused, told you will amount to nothing, you are a failure, raised in poverty, belittled), you are still valuable. You are valuable and you still have a purpose and something that this world needs and it's locked up in your potential. That is where your value is and no one can take that away from you.

Our purpose is linked to our potential

When we unlock the potential inside of us we open the door to purpose. We begin to fulfil what we were born to do. The potential that is inside of you is in the form of gifts, talent, ideas, dreams, imaginations, vision, desires, and aspirations.

Don't underestimate the gifts and talents that you were born with. Don't look down on the ideas that you have. I always say "It is better to live for an idea, than to live with an idea that will die". It is better to live out and pursue the idea that you have, than to let the idea die inside of you.

✓ Dr Myles Munroe once said the richest place on earth is not the gold and diamond mines of South Africa, the richest place on earth is the graveyard because buried beneath the soil are books that were not written, ideas that were not shared, songs that were not sung, and purpose that was not fulfilled.

✓ "Success knows your purpose in life, growing to reach your maximum potential and sowing seeds that benefit others." John Maxwell.

✓ Each and everyone one has got potential, we cannot afford to make the grave rich we need to unlock the potential inside and die empty.

Great Thoughts

- ☑ I am born with the potential to be great.
- ☑ I have a purpose in life.
- ☑ I have potential in the form of gifts, talent, ideas, dreams and aspirations.
- ☑ My potential is my key to greatness.

"Each and everyone one has got potential, we cannot afford to make the grave rich we need to unlock the potential inside and be GREAT"

Ambition Nugget: Write down or draw your ambition nugget from the topic

Self - Coaching Questions:

In the section below use each question to introspect, think and probe your answers further to incite action.

Goal, Reality, Explore, Action, Time Frame Questions	
GOAL	How can I discover my potential?

Goal, Reality, Explore, Action, Time Frame Questions	
REALITY	What have others noticed about my potential?

Goal, Reality, Explore, Action, Time Frame Questions	
EXPLORE	What can I do to discover my potential?

Goal, Reality, Explore, Action, Time Frame Questions	
ACTION	What steps must I take beginning today to start unlocking my potential?

Goal, Reality, Explore, Action, Time Frame Questions	
TIME FRAME	When will I start using my potential and how often?

2

DEVELOP REMARKABLE DREAMS

Your dreams can become a reality.

Every human being has the ability to dream. That is the most powerful key that you possess. No one can take that key away from you. One day you had a dream of starting your own business and that dream will or has become a reality.

If you can dream it you can do it.

Once your dream of completing High School is fulfilled, it's time to dream again. It will be time to dream new dreams. Dream of graduating with a degree, dream of buying your first car. Dream of travelling the world. Dream of starting your business. Dream of starting a new job. Dream of doing the impossible. So never stop dreaming!

Never let go of your dreams

There will be obstacles in achieving your dreams but never let go of those dreams. After matric my dream was to go to university and study dramatic arts but because there was no money for me to further my studies and go to university, I had to go and get a job. I started working when I was 18 years old. I only went to university fulltime 4 years after I completed my matric, at 22 years old. No matter how long the dream takes and the obstacles that may come your way don't give up on your dream. *A delay*

in accomplishing your dream is not a denial. It might take longer for you to accomplish it but don't give up on it.

The distance between your dreams and reality is called action

For your dream to come true you need to take action. Have clear goals that will help you to achieve your dream.

There used to be an advert on TV of this guy who was standing on a street corner with his friends. He would say to his friends, one day I am going to own a casino. They fast forwarded the ad to his life 10 years later. They showed him standing in the same spot with his friends still saying the same line, one day I am going to own a casino. Then they show him again 20 years later. He is still standing in the same corner saying one day I am going to own a casino. Though he had a dream, he did not take action in order for his dream to come true.

Great Thoughts

- ☑ I have the power to dream.
- ☑ My dream can become my reality.
- ☑ A delay in my dreams is not a denial.
- ☑ I must take action for my dreams to become a reality

"A dream without action is a wish, but a dream with action can make you REMARKABLE"

Ambition Nugget: Write down or draw your ambition nugget from the topic

Self- Coaching Reflections:

In the next section, use the coaching questions below to introspect, reflect and take action.

Goal, Reality, Explore, Action, Time Frame Questions	
GOAL	What are my 3 big dreams?

Goal, Reality, Explore, Action, Time Frame Questions	
REALITY	What challenges am I currently faced with that can hinder my dreams from becoming a reality?

Goal, Reality, Explore, Action, Time Frame Questions	
EXPLORE	What are the possible solutions to the challenges identified?

Goal, Reality, Explore, Action, Time Frame Questions	
ACTION	What actions do I commit to do that will help me to achieve my dreams?

Goal, Reality, Explore, Action, Time Frame Questions	
TIME FRAME	By when will I achieve this dream?

3

DEPLOY EXCEPTIONAL
SELF-DISCIPLINE

Discipline is the bridge between goals and achievement.

John Maxwell says, discipline is doing what you don't want in order to get what you want. If you want to pass with distinction (you do what you don't want, which is to study hard, in order to get what you want which is a distinction). If you want to lose weight you go to the gym which is what you don't want to do. But you keep going because you focus on the final result of weight loss. When you are disciplined you will achieve whatever you want to achieve. Discipline allows you to be exceptional.

Discipline says you pay now and play later.

When I was at university, I would go to the library every Friday evening. On my way there I would meet this one guy and he would ridicule me for going to the library on a Friday night. He would say its Friday people are going out to parties and clubs and I'm so boring for going to the library. He made fun of this every Friday for almost four years. But because I had a clear goal and was determined to finish my studies in the allocated time of the degree I pressed on. After four years of my degree I started working and bought a car. One day a friend invited me to her birthday party and asked if I could pick up a friend of hers from Wits University who needed a ride to the party. When I got to the university parking lot I was surprised to discover that the friend I was picking up was the same guy who had ridiculed me all those years before. He was still at university doing his first year of a new field of study. He had had to change his field of study several times because of failing different courses. So this was indeed proof that self-discipline pays. The principle of self-discipline says that you pay now and play later, there will always be parties and fun time, but there is time for everything under the sun. Learn to pay now and play later.

Goal setting is a tool of self-discipline.

When you set clear goals they will guide, shape your behavior and help you achieve your aspiration.

Your goals must be SMART – (Specific, Measurable, Attainable and Realistic and time bound)

If you just say I want to lose weight. The goal is not clear but if you say I want to lose 5kg by March 2020 by going to the gym every day for an hour and eating healthy and drinking 8 glasses of water. You are using smart principles. This goal is clear, specific and measurable.

Let's bring it closer home. For an example, saying "I want to pass Matric" is not a clear goal. But if you say I want to pass my matric with 4 distinctions by attending all my classes, forming a study group and going to the library on weekends. Framing your goal in this way is exceptional, and drives your behavior. Smart goals shapes your behavior and the friends that you hang around with, and guides you on how to spend your time wisely.

Great Thoughts

☑ I have to daily cross the bridge to being exceptional through self-discipline.
☑ I need to pay now in order to play later.
☑ I can use discipline to achieve greatness.
☑ SMART Goals can reinforce discipline in my life.

"EXCEPTIONAL people choose to be disciplined"

Ambition Nugget: Write down or draw your ambition nugget from the topic

Self-Coaching Questions:

In the next section, use the coaching questions below to introspect, reflect and take action.

Goal, Reality, Explore, Action, Time Frame	
	Questions
GOAL	What do I need to delay in order to achieve my goals?

Goal, Reality, Explore, Action, Time Frame Questions	
REALITY	What are the obstacles that are hindering me from applying self-discipline?

Goal, Reality, Explore, Action, Time Frame Questions	
EXPLORE	How can I reinforce discipline in my life?

Goal, Reality, Explore, Action, Time Frame Questions	
ACTION	What will it take for me to be more disciplined?

Goal, Reality, Explore, Action, Time Frame Questions	
TIME FRAME	What can I do daily to ritualize a disciplined life?

4

DECIDE TO MAKE AWESOME CHOICES

You always have a choice.

No one can violate your power of choice even God himself has given you the power of freewill and cannot take that power to choose away from you.

Victor Franklin once said between the stimulus and the response there is a gap and in the gap is our power to choose.

Every day when the sun rises you are faced with choices.

"You have the power to choose whether to wake up or stay in bed"

"You have the power to choose whether to be happy or moody"

"You have the power to choose whether to work hard or be lazy."

"You have power to choose whether to be friendly to others or rude."

Your choices reflect your hopes, not your fears - Nelson Mandela

Choice, not circumstances determines your success.

You cannot always choose what happens to you but you can choose how to respond. You did not choose the family that you were born in nor your upbringing but you can choose your future.

Yes, things happen to us like the illustration of the R100 note I shared earlier. But you still have a choice to rise above the ridicule, accusations, and negative words and respond differently. Life is a sum total of all your choices.

Your success is in your hands.

There was a young man who went to an old wise man and said to him; I have a bird in my hand, tell me if it's dead or alive. The old man answered him and said. If I tell you that the bird is dead you can squeeze it and it will die, but if I tell you that the bird is alive you can open your hand and let it go. The answer is in your hands.

✓ Your success is not dependent on your parents, your government or anyone else. Your success is your choice, and that choice lies in your hands.

✓ It only takes one person to change your life. That person is, YOU. Your success is in your hands.

✓ See you in the world of greatness.

✓ You were born to be Great Remarkable Exceptional Awesome Terrific

Great Thoughts

☑ No one can take my power of choice away from me.
☑ I cannot always choose what happens to me but I can choose how I respond.
☑ My success is my choice
☑ My success is in my hands.

Daily choices, not circumstance determines your AWESOME success!

Ambition Nugget: Write down or draw your ambition nugget from the topic

Self-Coaching Questions:

In the next section, use the coaching questions below to introspect, reflect and take action.

Goal, Reality, Explore, Action, Time Frame Questions	
GOAL	What choices do I need to make daily that can help me be successful?

Goal, Reality, Explore, Action, Time Frame Questions	
REALITY	What challenges am I faced with that make me feel powerless?

Goal, Reality, Explore, Action, Time Frame Questions	
EXPLORE	How can I use my power of choice effectively?

Goal, Reality, Explore, Action, Time Frame Questions	
ACTION	What action will I put in place to remind me of my power to choose?

Goal, Reality, Explore, Action, Time Frame Questions	
TIME FRAME	What am I going to do daily to use my power of choice effectively?

5

DOMINATE USING YOUR TERRIFIC TALENT

Potential is in all of us. When we use it, it grows and bears fruit. The fruits of potential are the gifts and talents inside of us that we need to discover and use in order to fulfill our purpose and be great.

Each one of us has been given talents and gifts that we are born with. According to oxford dictionary; a 'talent is a special ability or aptitude, a capacity for achievement or success. A gift can be defined as special ability or capacity; natural endowment; talent'. It is something bestowed or acquired without any particular effort by the recipient or without it being earned."

From the above definitions of talent and gifts it is clear that God has freely given us unearned natural, unique, abilities.

Things to note about your talent:

Every one of us has talent – each person has their own talent from God; one has this gift, another has that" We all have different gifts and talents according to the ability that God has given us.

1. Your talent is good and perfect

I remember my first year at University, after rigorous assessments, auditions and interviews I had finally made it to drama school. My first lecture was acting class and I was so looking forward to attending the class. After we had all walked in and sat on the floor, the lecturer opened with this statement, "if you are here and you want me to teach you how to act, please leave the room now". We all looked at each other confused. He repeated his statement and said, "I don't want to waste four years of your lives, please leave the room if you want me to teach you how to act? There was deafening silence in the room.

After some time, he looked at us and said, I am not here to teach you how to act but to shape the talent that is already inside of you, I will teach you techniques to enhance the talent, but not how to act, you are already actors.

In that same vein, the gift that you have is good and it's perfect, you did not learn or study it. It is natural and it comes already perfected. Your responsibility is to develop it and enhance it as the lecturer said. Imagine if we all went to university to develop and grow the talent we have instead of hoping that university will tell us if we are talented or not. If we choose careers that are in line with our gifts and talent, our work will be our play and we will never have to work a day in our life again.

2. Your talent is unique

Your talent is unique and different from anyone else's. There is a special way that we can use our talent that is different from others. You need to believe that your talent is different, only you can sing, cook, play sports, the way you do. Don't rob the world of your unique talent. No one has the same finger prints as you, in the same way your talent is unique to you.

3. Your talent is permanent

When God gives you a gift he does not take it away, it is with you until you die. You need to choose to develop and master it.

Don't hide it and think it's going to disappear. If you are a gifted singer, even when you are 90 years old you can still sing if you allow yourself to. Myles Munroe said to die with ability is irresponsible. Because your talent is permanent you are meant to use it to make a living with it. Your talent is meant to be your income.

Today people are celebrated singers, actors, lawyers, artists because they chose to develop and use their talents to make a living. You can choose that path too by choosing to be terrific in your talent.

There are many ways to discover what you are good at?

1. Think back to when you were a child, what were the things you considered hobbies?

2. Identify things you enjoy doing that people praise you for?

3. Things that you love doing, you feel fulfilled when you have done them?

4. Identify the things that come naturally that you do with ease that you never studied for?

5. Things that you don't mind doing for others?

6. Things that you can do for free?

Great Thoughts

☑ I am born with a talent
☑ My talent is unique and special

☑ My talent is permanent
☑ I need to develop and grow my terrific talent

Using your TERRIFIC talent will make room for you and bring you before great man.

Ambition Nugget: Write down or draw your ambition nugget from the topic

Self-Coaching Questions:

In the next section, use the coaching questions below to introspect, reflect and take action.

Goal, Reality, Explore, Action, Time Frame Questions	
GOAL	Identify 3 talents that you are good at?

Goal, Reality, Explore, Action, Time Frame Questions	
REALITY	How often do you use this talent?

Goal, Reality, Explore, Action, Time Frame Questions	
EXPLORE	How can you develop this talent?

Goal, Reality, Explore, Action, Time Frame Questions	
ACTION	**Where can you use the talent?**

Goal, Reality, Explore, Action, Time Frame Questions	
TIME FRAME	How often and when can you use this talent?

6

WHO IS HINDERING YOUR GREATNESS?

I would like to close this journey to greatness by sharing this story with you. One day all people were called into the community hall for a meeting. When they reached the hall, they saw a big notice on the gate on which it was written: Yesterday the person who has been hindering your growth in this community has passed away.

We invite you to join the funeral in the room that has been prepared in the hall. In the beginning they all got sad for the death of one of their neighbors, or someone they all know. But after a while they started getting curious to know, who was that man who hindered the growth of his community and the society? The excitement in the hall was such that police were ordered to control the crowd within the room.

Who is this guy who was hindering their progress?

Well at least he died!

The more people reached the coffin, the more the noise heated up.

There was a mirror inside the coffin.

There is only one person who is capable to sets limits to your growth, that person is YOU!

You are the only person who can revolutionize your life.

You are the only person who can influence your happiness.

You are the only person who can help yourself.

Your life does not change, when you government changes.

Your life does not change when your parents change.

Your life changes when you change.

When you go beyond your limiting beliefs.

When you realize that you are the only one responsible for your life. Examine yourself, watch yourself, and handle yourself well in front of others. Don't be afraid of difficulties, impossibilities and losses.

Be a winner; build yourself and your reality

The most important relationship you can have is the one you have with yourself.

Write down your commitment of how you are going to unlock your potential, fulfil your purpose and be GREAT.

Your commitment:

Signature: _____   Date: _____

REFERENCES

1. Munroe, M. revised edition. 2002, 2005. Understanding Purpose. Destiny Image. Bahamas
2. Maxwell, J. C, 2012 The 15 Invaluable laws of Growth. Grad Central. Publishing. USA
3. Who is hindering your growth modified version: Author Unknown